from SPANISH to PORTUGUESE

Jack L. Ulsh

An Audio Course. Specially created to accompany this book are 2 instructional CDs or cassettes. They are available from the publisher.

FOREIGN SERVICE INSTITUTE
DEPARTMENT OF STATE

AUDIO·FORUM
a division of Jeffrey Norton Publishers, Inc.
Madison, Connecticut

From Spanish to Portuguese

ISBN: 0-88432-645-4   text only
       1-57970-210-4   text and CDs
       0-88432-059-6   text and cassettes

This printing produced by Audio-Forum
a division of Jeffrey Norton Publishers, Inc.
One Orchard Park Road, Madison CT 06443 USA

Printed in the United States of America

PREFACE

From Spanish to Portuguese is designed to provide help and guidance to native speakers of American English who have a good command of Spanish and want to acquire a knowledge of Portuguese. The manual focuses on features of Portuguese pronunciation, grammar and vocabulary that have similar but not always identical counterparts in Spanish. The correspondences are sometimes deceptive, with the result that they can create difficulties and interference when the learner attempts to transfer to Portuguese what seems to be a similar form in Spanish. The text helps learners overcome this kind of difficulty by pointing out the distinctions in corresponding patterns of the two languages.

The recordings, which illustrate the features of spoken Portuguese included in the text, were made in the studio of the Foreign Service Institute Language Laboratory with the technical assistance of Jose M. Ramirez and under the general supervision of Gary Alley. The Portuguese voicing was supplied by R. Victor dos Reis. The typescript was prepared by Irma C. Ponce.

> James R. Frith, Dean
> School of Language Studies
> Foreign Service Institute

FROM SPANISH TO PORTUGUESE

FROM SPANISH TO PORTUGUESE

TABLE OF CONTENTS

Author's Foreword v
Special Note on Cognates viii

Part I THE SOUNDS

The Vowels 1

  Spanish Vowels with Counterparts in Portuguese 1

    1. Spanish a / Portuguese a 1
    2. Spanish unstressed o and e / Portuguese unstressed u and i 4

  Portuguese Vowels Not Occurring in Spanish 8

    1. Oral Vowels 8
    2. Nasal Vowels 13

The Diphthongs 16

  Spanish Diphthongs with Counterparts in Portuguese 16
  Portuguese Diphthongs Not Occurring in Spanish 17

    1. Oral Diphthongs 17
    2. Nasal Diphthongs 18

  Diphthongs Restricted to Some Dialects 20

The Consonants 21

  Spanish Consonants with Counterparts in Portuguese 21
  Portuguese Consonants Not Occurring in Spanish 26
  Observations on Major Brazilian Dialect Differences ... 28
  Consonant Clusters 28

Part II THE GRAMMAR

Introduction 29
Word Order 31

  Word Order in Questions with Interrogative Words 31
  Word Order in Yes-No Questions 32
  Word Order in Answers to Yes-No Questions 32

Negation 34

  An Extra Negative 34
  Portuguese 'either/neither' 34

FROM SPANISH TO PORTUGUESE

Contractions 35
Verbs 39

Verb Types 39
Regular Verb Forms 39
Irregular Verb Forms 44
Verb Constructions 46

1. Spanish (ir + a + infinitive) vs. Portuguese
   (ir + infinitive) 46
2. Spanish (haber + past participle) vs. Portuguese
   (ter + past participle)................................. 47
3. Spanish gustar vs. Portuguese gostar de 48
4. Spanish hacer vs. Portuguese haver in time expressions 48
5. Spanish (estar + -ndo) vs. Portuguese (estar + a + infinitive) 49

Usage of ser and estar 49
Two New Verb Categories 51

1. Future Subjunctive 51
2. Personal Infinitive 52

Nominals 57

Object Pronouns 57

1. Placement 57
2. Other Problems 60

Direct Object Nouns 63
Definite Article 63
Gender 64

1. In Cognates 64
2. In the Number 'Two' 64

Part III   HINTS ON VOCABULARY TRANSFER

Some Patterns of Correspondences 65

Common Correspondences 65

1. Sounds 65
2. Word Endings 73

Less Common Correspondences 75

False Cognates 80

Part IV

SUPPLEMENTARY PRONUNCIATION EXERCISES 81

FROM SPANISH TO PORTUGUESE

AUTHOR'S FOREWORD

Introduction

If you are like most Americans who already speak Spanish and who are now about to learn Portuguese, you want to know whether your Spanish will help you or hinder you. You want to know whether it will be an advantage or a disadvantage, an asset or a liability. Since Spanish and Portuguese are so close, your first inclination is to assume that the transition from one to the other will be quite easy. But you cannot wholly accept this idea, because friends who have already made the transition have told you that your Spanish will interfere with your Portuguese. They have warned you to expect considerable difficulty in keeping your Spanish out of your Portuguese. You contrast these remarks with the more favorable comments of other friends who have also gone from Spanish to Portuguese. They tell you how easy it was. It is quite understandable, then, that you are not sure what to believe.

We who supervise Portuguese instruction at the Foreign Service Institute have observed that the majority of students who already speak Spanish make better progress in Portuguese than those who do not. Although the Spanish they know so well makes frequent and unwanted intrusions on their Portuguese, it also gives them considerable insight into the new language. So much of what was learned in Spanish is now applicable to Portuguese. Our conclusion is that the advantages of this transfer factor far outweigh the disadvantages of interference. We feel that Spanish is a distinct asset. If _you_ have wondered about the utility of your Spanish in this new venture, and particularly if you have already started Portuguese instruction and have found yourself blocked by Spanish at every step, take heart! You will soon see that you have much more going _for_ you than _against_ you.

FROM SPANISH TO PORTUGUESE

Spanish and Portuguese long ago separated from a common ancestor and became identifiable as two distinct languages, but they are still close enough to each other to enable us to use the word 'conversion' when describing what the speaker of one language does in order to achieve command of the other. An American speaker of Spanish cannot help but go through a kind of conversion process in his approach to Portuguese. His mind will not let him do otherwise, for he is constantly reminded of the many correspondences between the two languages, of the many areas where they are parallel or nearly parallel. Inevitably and logically he sees the primary task before him to be that of altering his Spanish patterns so as to fit the Portuguese mold. He is going to get at Portuguese via Spanish. He is going to convert.

This manual has grown out of a need to supply students with a guide to making the Spanish to Portuguese conversion. It is written in a casual, informal style, not unlike the conversational style of the classroom, where much of its content had its origin and initial expression. It is written for you, the student. It provides an extensive, non-technical examination of those Spanish/Portuguese correspondences that have proven most troublesome to students, correspondences which you must be particularly aware of if you wish to keep your Portuguese separate from your Spanish. This manual is not exhaustive in its approach; it does not attempt to cover all the differences between the two languages. It concentrates on the known trouble spots.

The terminology used in this manual takes the conversion process into account. It recognizes the fact that in going from Spanish to Portuguese you will see the latter in terms of the former. You will compare nearly everything you learn in Portuguese with its counterpart in Spanish. The word 'conversion' is itself a reflection of this frame of mind. When we talk about 'changing' or 'modifying' Spanish patterns, when we say that a Spanish sound

FROM SPANISH TO PORTUGUESE

'drops out' of its Portuguese counterpart, or when we speak of a 'new' Portuguese sound, we are echoing the thoughts of students before you. We are using terminology which reflects the point of view of the American who is using Spanish as a springboard to Portuguese.

An attempt to examine the distinctions between European and Brazilian Portuguese is beyond the scope of this manual. In any case, such treatment would not be particularly useful to us, since the special problems of the Spanish speaker are much the same regardless of which kind of Portuguese he is learning. On the assumption that the majority of users will be studying standard Brazilian Portuguese, I have elected to write about this variety. However, students of European Portuguese will find that this manual has nearly as much to offer them as it does to those who are studying Brazilian Portuguese.

The manual is divided into four parts: 'The Sounds', 'The Grammar', 'Vocabulary Transfer', and 'Supplementary Pronunciation Exercises'. We recommend that you read about the sounds and do the pronunciation exercises at the very beginning of your Portuguese course, for it is then that you will experience most of your interference from Spanish pronunciation. You may want to read the other two parts in their entirety at any time, but we especially recommend that you select for careful study the various subsections of these two parts at such time as they fit in with the course of study you are following. The Portuguese portions of all four parts are available on tape.

Many of my colleagues have contributed in various ways to the preparation of this manual. While I cannot name them all, I do want to give special credit to Dr. Earl Stevick and Miss Madeline E. Ehrman, both of whom read the original manuscript and offered many useful suggestions.

FROM SPANISH TO PORTUGUESE

Special Note on Cognates

Spanish and Portuguese share a huge quantity of words. We will refer to these shared words as cognates, words that are easily recognizable from one language to another.

Probably upwards of 85 per cent of Portuguese vocabulary consists of words which have a cognate in Spanish. Sometimes the difference in cognates is not great, as, for example, the slight change in vowel qualities that you will notice between Spanish bonito and Portuguese bonito. At other times the difference may be quite pronounced, but the word will still be readily recognizable. Consider, for example, Portuguese agora, vs. Spanish ahora, and Portuguese chover vs. Spanish llover. Rather drastic sound changes have been introduced in the Portuguese words, but you should still recognize them as words which have a first cousin in Spanish.

Cognates will be used frequently on the following pages to illustrate certain correspondences between Spanish and Portuguese. You are likely to get the impression from time to time that every Spanish word has a Portuguese cognate. You should not let yourself think this. Some of the most common words of Portuguese do not have a cognate in Spanish. As a rule it is difficult to predict their occurrence. You can appreciate this by studying the following examples.

a. Portuguese amanhã and hoje are cognates for Spanish mañana and hoy. Knowing this, you might expect the Portuguese word for 'yesterday' to be a cognate too. It is not. It is ontem, which does not resemble ayer in the slightest.

FROM SPANISH TO PORTUGUESE

b. You will readily recognize Portuguese _camisa_, _blusa_, and _sapato_, since you already know these words in Spanish. You are not likely, however, to know what _saia_ is until somebody or something tells you. It is the word for 'skirt', and it obviously is far removed from the familiar Spanish _falda_.

Cognates do often fall into recognizable patterns (as shown later in Part III, 'Vocabulary Transfer'), but it is very difficult to be sure that you will find a cognate in a given case. You must learn which words from your Spanish inventory have cognates and which do not.

FROM SPANISH TO PORTUGUESE

PART I

THE SOUNDS

In this section we will compare the sounds of Spanish with the sounds of Portuguese. We will illustrate our comments with cognates in order to help you transfer vocabulary items from Spanish into Portuguese.

The Vowels

Spanish Vowels with Counterparts in Portuguese

You will recall that Spanish has just five vowels, a e i o and u. These same five familiar vowel sounds, pronounced essentially as you know them in Spanish, occur frequently in Portuguese, but they are interspersed with seven additional vowel sounds, new ones that do not exist in Spanish. The existence of these seven additional vowels and their several diphthongs means that you must now learn to operate within a more extensive vowel system. It also means that you will have to exercise considerable caution in transferring the five Spanish vowels, particularly in cognates. You cannot do so as freely as you would like, as you will discover on these pages.

In addition to accommodating yourself to the seven new vowels, you will also need to learn to handle some very common variations of the familiar a, e and o. These variations occur for the most part when these vowels occur at the ends of words and are unstressed. We discuss each of these in turn below.

1. Spanish a / Portuguese ǝ

The Portuguese a has a special variant, not occurring in Spanish, which will probably cause you some problems during your early days of study. We will arbitrarily elect to write this

FROM SPANISH TO PORTUGUESE

variant for the moment like this: ə. It is similar to a common English vowel sound, the sort of lax, neutral 'uh'-type sound that you and all native-speakers of English say in the final, weak-stressed syllable of words like 'sofa', 'comma', 'Anna', 'abbot', when you utter these words in a normal, unaffected way. In your early days of learning Spanish you had to break away from this comfortable English habit and force yourself not to use this sound in the final, weak-stressed syllable of Spanish words. You had to learn to say a, and not ə, in the last syllable of casa, toma, señoras, ganan, and many other words.

Now, in Portuguese, you will find that this sound does occur, and with great frequency, in final, weak-stressed syllables. For example, you will hear it in the last syllable of Portuguese casa, toma, senhoras, which is precisely where you learned not to use it in the corresponding Spanish words. It will be in just such easily recognizable Portuguese/Spanish cognate words as these, where the final unstressed vowel in Spanish is a, that you will need to be particularly careful to use the Portuguese ə. It requires a bit of undoing of a familiar and comfortable pattern. Below are a few cases in point.

Spanish (weak-stressed a is underlined.)	Portuguese (spelling is altered to show weak-stressed ə.)
cas<u>a</u>	casə
señor<u>a</u>s	senhorəs
par<u>a</u>	parə
dí<u>a</u>s	diəs
ahor<u>a</u>	agorə
nad<u>a</u>	nadə
cabez<u>a</u>	cabeçə
tom<u>a</u>	tomə

2

FROM SPANISH TO PORTUGUESE

Of course the ə occurs in the final, weak-stressed syllable of many non-cognate words as well. Here, too, you will have to resist the tendency to use a Spanish a.

falə	ficə
obrigadə	feirə

It is interesting to note that in European Portuguese and in the rapid speech of some Brazilians there is a definite tendency to pass over this sound very lightly, sometimes to the point of dropping it.

The ə is also heard in stressed syllables when the following syllable begins with m, n or nh sound. In these cases the ə is slightly nasalized. Once again, interference from familiar, cognate Spanish words is likely to be a problem.

Spanish (a)	Portuguese (ə)
vamos	vəmos
cama	cəmə
baño	bənho
gano	gənho
Ana	ənə

The differences between Spanish a and Portuguese ə may not seem very great, but it is on just such small differences as these—hundreds of them—that Spanish and Portuguese are distinguishable as two separate languages.

Merely as an indication of the considerable frequency with which you will need to perform this a to ə change, we have tabulated its presence below in some very basic, hence constantly recurring, grammatical features of the two languages.

FROM SPANISH TO PORTUGUESE

Frequency check: Spanish a / Portuguese ə

The Spanish unstressed a sound marks many feminine nouns and their agreeing adjectives (casa bonita, etc.), the third person singular present tense of -ar verbs (manda, vuela, etc.), and the singular subjunctives of -er and -ir verbs (viva, sepa, etc.). In Portuguese, you will find ə in these positions.

	Spanish	Portuguese
Nouns:	casa	casə
	señoras	senhorəs
	para	parə
	días	diəs
Adjectives:	bonita	bonitə
	cara	carə

Verbs: (3rd person singular, present tense of -ar verbs)

	toma	tomə
	manda	mandə
	trabaja	trabalhə

(singular subjunctive of -er, -ir verbs)

	aprenda	aprendə
	coma	comə

2. Spanish unstressed o and e / Portuguese unstressed u and i

Spanish very commonly ends a word with an unstressed o or an unstressed e sound (como, baño, sale, vive, etc.) Since you are accustomed to using these two sounds at the ends of words in Spanish you will find that you will want to use them in this position in Portuguese, too, especially if you are dealing with

FROM SPANISH TO PORTUGUESE

cognates. In very careful, overly precise speech a Portuguese speaker may occasionally end words with the unstressed o and e sounds of his own language, but in normal, everyday speech he will always use u and i sounds, respectively, instead. These two features of Portuguese speech will be among the first to strike your ears. The frequency check presented below will indicate how often you will be required to focus on them.

Frequency check: (Spanish o / Portuguese u)

In Spanish the unstressed o sound marks many masculine nouns and their agreeing adjectives (carro viejo, etc.) as well as the first person singular, present tense of most verbs (tengo, llevo, etc.) In Portuguese, these functions are taken over by the unstressed u sound (which, nonetheless, is written o in standard spelling). Observe the change in the examples shown below, all cognates. We have altered the standard Portuguese spelling to emphasize the presence of the u sound.

	Spanish	Portuguese
Nouns:	carro	carru
	centro	centru
	estados	estadus
	libros	livrus
Adjectives:	cuatro	quatru
	famoso	famosu
	bonitos	bonitus
	caros	carus

FROM SPANISH TO PORTUGUESE

Verbs: (first person singular, present tense):

    tom**o**   tom**u**
    llev**o**   lev**u**
    teng**o**   tenh**u**
    viv**o**   viv**u**

Frequency check: (Spanish **e** / Portuguese **i**)

In Spanish, an unstressed **e** sound marks the 3rd person singular of most **-er** and **-ir** verbs (aprend**e**, sal**e**, etc.), and the singular subjunctive of most **-ar** verbs (mand**e**, trabaj**e**, etc.). It also occurs frequently as the last vowel in nouns and adjectives (hombr**e** grand**e**, billet**e** verd**e**), etc.

In Portuguese these functions are assumed by the unstressed **i** sound (which, nonetheless, is written **e** in standard spelling, just as it is in Spanish). Compare these sample cognates. We have altered the Portuguese spelling to emphasize the presence of the unstressed **i** sound.

            Spanish   Portuguese

Verbs: (3rd person singular, **-er**, **-ir** verbs)

    aprend**e**   aprend**i**
    abr**e**   abr**i**
    muev**e**   mov**i**
    cab**e**   cab**i**

(singular subjunctive of **-ar** verbs)

    habl**e**   fal**i**
    mand**e**   mand**i**
    pas**e**   pass**i**

FROM SPANISH TO PORTUGUESE

Adjectives:	grand_e_	grand_i_
	verd_e_	verd_i_
	es_e_	ess_i_
Nouns:	bas_e_	bas_i_
	noch_e_	noit_i_
	tard_e_	tard_i_
	billet_e_	bilhet_i_

The shift from Spanish unstressed _e_ to Portuguese unstressed _i_ is evident elsewhere too. For example, many Portuguese speakers have the initial unstressed syllables _is-_ and _dis-_ where your Spanish experience would lead you to expect the unstressed _es-_ and _des-_.

Spanish	Portuguese (spelling altered to show _i_ sound)
_e_sperar	_i_sperar
_e_star	_i_star
_e_sposo	_i_sposo
_e_scribir	_i_screver
de_s_cuido	di_s_cuido
de_s_dén	di_s_dém
de_s_tino	di_s_tino

Additional practice with unstressed _ə_, _u_ and _i_ is found in Part IV, exercises 1, 2 and 3.

FROM SPANISH TO PORTUGUESE

Portuguese Vowels Not Occurring in Spanish

Portuguese has seven vowels that do not occur in Spanish. For examination purposes we can divide these new vowels into two groups: oral vowels and nasal vowels.

1. Oral Vowels

We will look at the new oral vowels first. There are two of them. Since they are somewhat difficult to identify in standard spelling we have chosen to write them for the moment like this: E, O. (The use of capitals is deliberate.)

A. <u>The oral vowel E</u>.

This vowel is somewhat similar to the vowel in the English words **bet** and **set**. To produce it, one must have a somewhat larger opening between the tongue and the roof of the mouth than one needs to produce the e. Perhaps for this reason it is sometimes referred to as the 'open' E, in contrast to the e, which in turn may be called 'closed'. Be careful, however, not to think of E as just a variation of the Portuguese e. It is another vowel altogether, as different from e as a is from o. Notice the difference the 'open' E makes in the following pairs of words.

With 'closed' e		With 'open' E	
êste	(this)	Este	(east)
sêlo	(stamp)	sElo	(I seal, stamp)
gêlo	(ice)	gElo	(I freeze)
cêrro	(hill)	cErro	(I close)
sêde	(thirst)	sEde	(headquarters)
sexta	(sixth)	sEsta	(nap, siesta)

FROM SPANISH TO PORTUGUESE

Inevitably some interference will arise out of the necessity of accommodating two vowel sounds in an area where you are used to dealing with only one. This will be a problem in the case of brand new, non-cognate words. It will be even more of a problem in the case of cognates. Many Spanish words with e (which we may consider closed) will show up in Portuguese with the open E. Among these are Spanish words ending in stressed -el.

Spanish	Portuguese
papel	papEl
pincel	pincEl
hotel	hotEl

In most cases, though, you will find it difficult to predict whether you will find an e or an E in the Portuguese word. Check these examples:

Spanish closed e	Portuguese closed e	Portuguese open E
pelo	pelo	
mesa	mesa	
pena	pena	
pelar	pelar	
tenaz	tenaz	
menos	menos	
mero		mEro
sede		sEde
bella		bEla
fe		fÉ
ella		Ela
es		É
cero		zEro
flecha		flEcha

FROM SPANISH TO PORTUGUESE

Let us look at this E in another environment. You remember that Spanish has a lot of words containing the diphthong _ie_. Most of these (a rough estimate would put the figure at 95 per cent) show up in Portuguese with the open vowel E. Although this change may be annoying to you because of the interference factor, you will find that it is a very useful device to keep in mind, simply because it is applicable to so many words. We are listing just a few of them here.

Spanish	Portuguese
siete	sEte
ciego	cEgo
piedra	pEdra
piel	pEle
miel	mEl
tierra	tErra
pierde	pErde
pie	pÊ
fiesta	fEsta
diez	dEz

If Spanish _ie_ is followed by n or m in the same syllable, as in **siempre**, the vowel in the Portuguese cognate word will most likely be the nasal vowel ẽ. (See page 13.) It will not be the open E.

B. **The oral vowel O**.

The other new oral vowel is O, often called 'open' O. Once again we can apply the term 'open' to refer to the fact that there is more space —more of an 'opening'— between tongue and roof-of-mouth for this vowel (the O) than for the o. The o, in turn, is often referred to as 'closed'. The 'closed' o is very similar to the Spanish o.

FROM SPANISH TO PORTUGUESE

The o and O are quite different and quite separate vowels in Portuguese. Here are several pairs of words which will illustrate this.

With closed o (as underlined)		With open O	
avô	(grandfather)	avó	(grandmother)
côro	(chorus)	cOro	(I blush)
almôço	(lunch)	almOço	(I eat lunch)
gôsto	(taste)	gOsto	(I like)
pôço	(well)	pOsso	(I can)

Just as you will have some trouble learning the distribution of e and E, so you will also have trouble learning the distribution of o and O. When is it one and when is it the other? Again, the answer seems to be: Take each word as it comes along, and learn it. Of course, your well-established habit of saying a closed Spanish o will tempt you to carry this sound over into Portuguese too, particularly in cognates. In the case of some cognates, you will be right, as these examples show.

Spanish closed o	Portuguese closed o
gota	gôta
boca	bôca
mozo	môço
como	como
boba	boba
popular	popular
noticia	notícia

But in the case of many other cognates you will have to switch to the open O, as the following examples show.

11

FROM SPANISH TO PORTUGUESE

Spanish closed o	Portuguese open o
nOta	nOta
mOda	mOda
nOrte	nOrte
obvio	óbvio
bOta	bOta

As you can see, there does not appear to be any pattern you can follow.

Spanish has a large number of words that contain the diphthong ue. Many, but not all, of these show up in Portuguese with the open o.

Spanish	Portuguese
fuerte	fOrte
luego	lOgo
cuerda	cOrda
puerta	pOrta
nueve	nOve
rueda	rOda
muerte	mOrte
escuela	escOla
puede	pOde
suelo	sOlo

Spanish puerto and hueso, however, show up as porto and osso, both containing the closed o. So you will have to be careful not to assume that every Spanish ue will turn out to be an open o in Portuguese. It is, nonetheless, a good rule of thumb. And, if the Spanish ue is followed by an m or n in the same syllable, as in cuenta, the Portuguese cognate will most likely have the nasal vowel õ, as in cõta. (See page 13.)

FROM SPANISH TO PORTUGUESE

For additional occurrences of both the o and the e sounds see the sub-division on 'Irregular Verb Forms', pages 44-46.

2. Nasal Vowels

You know, of course, that Spanish has no such thing as a nasal vowel. Nor does English, for that matter. So the process of pronouncing a vowel 'through your nose', as the saying goes, may be new to you. Rest assured, though, that it is not a particularly difficult thing for most people to learn to do.

Portuguese has five nasal vowels. They are:

ẽ ĩ õ ũ and ã

In our modified spelling we will use the tilde (~). In standard spelling, nasal vowels are frequently signalled by the presence of an m or n after the vowel in the same syllable, as in <u>vendo</u>, <u>sim</u>, <u>bom</u>, <u>ums</u>, and <u>banda</u>. In addition, the tilde designates many õ and ã sounds (the latter being written ã).

It is important to remember that these nasal vowels are not mere variations of their non-nasal, or oral, counterparts. They are completely different vowels, every bit as distinct from the non-nasals as a is from o and as i is from u.

The nasal vowels show up frequently in easily recognizable Spanish/Portuguese cognate words. In the Spanish version of these words, you first pronounce the vowel, then you pronounce an m or n sound. In Portuguese, however, you simply nasalize the vowel. That's all. You do not pronounce an m or an n. If you do, nobody will have any trouble understanding you, but your Portuguese will be more Spanish than you should want it to be. Be alert then to the changes you will have to make in such cognate items as the following:

13

FROM SPANISH TO PORTUGUESE

Spanish a	Portuguese nasal ɐ̃	
cuando	quando	(quɐ̃du)
cuanto	quanto	(quɐ̃tu)
banco	banco	(bɐ̃cu)
cantar	cantar	(cɐ̃tar)
mandar	mandar	(mɐ̃dar)
andando	andando	(ɐ̃dɐ̃du)

(and other -ndo forms of -ar verbs)

Spanish e	Portuguese nasal ẽ	
senda	senda	(sẽdə)
vencer	vencer	(vẽcer)
mentir	mentir	(mẽtir)
vender	vender	(vẽder)
aprendiendo	aprendendo	(aprẽdẽdu)

(and other -ndo forms of -er verbs)

Spanish i	Portuguese nasal ĩ	
fin	fim	(fĩ)
pintar	pintar	(pĩtar)
insulto	insulto	(ĩsultu)
importante	importante	(ĩportɐ̃ti)
dirigiendo	dirigindo	(dirigĩdu)

(and other -ndo forms of -ir verbs.)

FROM SPANISH TO PORTUGUESE

Spanish o   Portuguese nasal õ

responder   responder   (respõder)
montaña   montanha   (mõntenha)
donde   onde   (õdi)
onza   onça   (õçe)
onda   onda   (õde)

Spanish u   Portuguese nasal ũ

fundar   fundar   (fũdar)
tumba   tumba   (tũbe)
mundo   mundo   (mũdu)

15

FROM SPANISH TO PORTUGUESE

The Diphthongs

Spanish Diphthongs with Counterparts in Portuguese

Most of the diphthongs that occur in Spanish also occur in Portuguese, but with different degrees of frequency. We will not bother to treat all of them here, but will make just a few comments about several of them.

Spanish _ie_ and _ue_ can be found in Portuguese, but not nearly so often as in Spanish. We have already seen that the Portuguese open _e_ and open _o_ sounds frequently appear when you are accustomed to hearing Spanish _ie_ and _ue_.

On the other hand, the diphthongs _ei_ and _eu_, which are somewhat limited in their occurrence in Spanish, are very common in Portuguese.

You should be particularly mindful of the _ei_, since it often appears in those positions where Spanish has a simple _e_ sound. When this is the case, you will have to be doubly careful to add the '-i-glide' to the _e_ sound and make it a genuine diphthong. It will sound much like the -_ay_ of English _bay_. Compare these examples:

Spanish	Portuguese
quemar	queimar
dejar	deixar
madera	madeira
manera	maneira
primero	primeiro
verdadero	verdadeiro
caballero	cavalheiro
dinero	dinheiro
soltero	solteiro

Notice that many of these Spanish words end in _ero_ and _era_.

The _ei_ diphthong is also to be found in these verb endings:

  mand_ei_, mandar_ei_   (cf. Spanish mand_é_, mandar_é_)
  fal_ei_, falar_ei_   (cf. Spanish habl_é_, hablar_é_)
  cant_ei_, cantar_ei_   (cf. Spanish cant_é_, cantar_é_)

and others of the sort. (See exercise 7, Part IV.)

The most common occurrences of the _eu_ diphthong are:

a. meu, seu   (cf. Spanish m_i_, s_u_)
b. eu   (cf. Spanish y_o_)
c. deus, adeus   (cf. Spanish d_ios_, ad_iós_)
d. (the 3rd person, singular, past tense ending of regular -_er_ verbs)

  venceu   (cf. Spanish venc_ió_)
  valeu   (cf. Spanish val_ió_)
  bebeu   (cf. Spanish beb_ió_)
  comeu   (cf. Spanish com_ió_)
  vendeu   (cf. Spanish vend_ió_)

Portuguese Diphthongs Not Occurring in Spanish

1. Oral Diphthongs

Among the new diphthongs are three involving the open vowel sounds _E_ and _O_.

  _Ei_, as in pap_éis_, hot_éis_
  _Eu_, as in c_éu_, chap_éu_
  _Oi_, as in d_ói_, her_ói_

Also new is _ou_, as in v_ou_, s_ou_. Note particularly its presence in trabalh_ou_, fal_ou_, mand_ou_ and similar past tense items where Spanish has the single vowel -_ó_ (cf. Spanish trabaj_ó_, habl_ó_, mand_ó_).

FROM SPANISH TO PORTUGUESE

2. **Nasal Diphthongs**

The nasal vowels ã, ẽ, and õ combine with the vowel sounds i and u to form four nasal diphthongs:

ãi, as in mãe, cães, pães
ẽi, (usually spelled em), as in vem, tem, bem, dizem
õi, as in põe, canções, botões, funções
ãu, as in não, pão, falam, saíram

(A fifth diphthong, ũi, appears only in the word muito.)

The ãu diphthong is very useful. It corresponds to the Spanish verb endings -án, -an, and -on. It also corresponds to Spanish noun endings -ón and -ión. Observe the samples below. Additional practice is available in exercises 4, 5 and 6, Part IV.

a. Third person plural verb forms:

Spanish	Portuguese (spelling)
pasan	passam
pasaban	passavam
pasarán	passarão
pasarían	passariam
pasaron	passaram
van	vão
dan	dão
digan	digam
reciban	recebam
están	estão
son	são

b. Nouns:

limón	limão
melón	melão
montón	montão

18

FROM SPANISH TO PORTUGUESE

salón   salão
corazón   coração
condición   condição
destinación   destinação
sección   seção
lección   lição

(Many other nouns ending in -ón and -ión in Spanish will end in the diphthong -ãu in Portuguese.)

c. Others:

tan   tão
san   são

The õi diphthong is heard in the common plural ending -ões, which corresponds to Spanish -ones and -iones. Compare these Spanish and Portuguese plurals of nouns listed in (b) above.

Spanish	Portuguese
limones	limões
melones	melões
montones	montões
salones	salões
corazones	corações
condiciones	condições
destinaciones	destinações
secciones	seções
lecciones	lições

The ẽi diphthong often corresponds to the Spanish verb-ending -en. Compare:

Spanish	Portuguese (spelling)
viven	vivem
venden	vendem
manden	mandem
viviesen	vivessem

19

Diphthongs Restricted to Some Dialects

It is striking to the ears of Spanish speakers that in the speech of many Brazilians a stressed vowel before a final s sound is glided toward the i sound. The result is a diphthong.

Standard Spelling	Possible Pronunciation
gás	[gais]
mas 'but'	[mais]
arroz	[arrois]
nós	[nois]
feroz	[ferois]
eficaz	[eficais]
vez	[veis]
luz	[luis]
pus	[puis]
avestruz	[avestruis]
voz	[vois]
maçãs	[maçãis]
irmãs	[irmãis]
manhãs	[manhãis]

FROM SPANISH TO PORTUGUESE

The Consonants

Spanish Consonants with Counterparts in Portuguese

You can carry the following Spanish consonant sounds over into Portuguese with little or no modification.

 b*   d*   g*   p   t   k   (of como)   f   s   m   n   r   (of pero)

*A special word needs to be said about the b, d and g sounds starred above. These symbols refer only to the often-called 'hard' varieties of these sounds, as heard in bien, donde and gano when these words occur first in an utterance. Portuguese does not have the 'soft' varieties of these sounds that occur between Spanish vowels and certain other places in that language.

Presumably you remember what is meant by 'soft' and 'hard' in this context. You probably know, for example, that the d of Spanish nada is considerably 'softer' than either d of donde. It is something like the th of English 'this'. Sometimes the Spanish speaker seems to pass over it so lightly, so softly, that it all but disappears, and you hear something which we might write as na'a. None of this ever happens in Portuguese. The d of the Portuguese word nada is a firm—a 'hard'—d sound much as we English speakers understand and recognize a d sound.

Likewise, the b of Spanish suba is considered to be a soft sound, since the speaker's lips do not close all the way during its production. But in the Portuguese word suba the lips are closed all the way on the b sound and the result is a sound which is very nearly the same as our familiar English b sound.

The same comparison can be drawn with regard to the g. Observe, for example, the difference between the slightly soft g of Spanish pago and the harder g of Portuguese pago.

FROM SPANISH TO PORTUGUESE

So, to summarize, you will always want to use the hard varieties of b, d and g in Portuguese, never the soft.

You will experience most of your trouble with easily recognizable cognate words. Below are a few samples.[1] The Spanish spelling has been slightly altered to show the soft b, d and g sounds.

Spanish		Portuguese
nada		nada
boda		boda
ida		ida
seda		sêda
mudar		mudar
formado	(And many other such participial forms)	formado
comido		comido
lobo		lôbo
Cuba		Cuba
saber		saber
sábado		sábado
caber		caber
entregar		entregar
pegar		pegar
digo		digo
pago		pago

Some Spanish consonants have counterparts in Portuguese which, though similar, are different enough to warrant special attention. We treat them below.

---

[1] Extensive practice on b and d can be found in exercises 9 and 10, Part IV.

FROM SPANISH TO PORTUGUESE

1. Spanish __rr__ / Portuguese __rr__ (indicated here as __R__).

Portuguese has a counterpart of the Spanish multiple trilled __rr__. For most Portuguese speakers the trilling is produced in the back of the mouth with the uvula, rather than in the front of the mouth with the tongue tip. In the speech of many Brazilians, particularly from the Rio area, the sound is much like a slightly hoarse Spanish or English __h__ sound with perhaps a bit of vocalization added. For others it more nearly resembles the voiced French __r__. Your best bet, of course, will be to imitate your native-speaking instructor.

The __R__ appears where your Spanish experience would lead you to expect it. Check below and in Part IV, exercise 13.

    a. Initially   (__R__oupa, __R__uim)

    b. Between vowels (ca__R__o, ga__R__afa)

    c. Finally   (senho__R__, come__R__)

You should be particularly careful about this sound in familiar cognate words, a few of which are given below.

	Spanish	Portuguese
a.	ropa	Roupa
	revista	Revista
	rápido	Rápido
	río	Rio
	ropita	Ropita
	razón	Rasão
b.	carro	caRo
	arroz	aRoz
	corre	coRe
	guerra	gueRa
	torre	toRe

23

FROM SPANISH TO PORTUGUESE

c. señor   senhoR
    placer   prazeR
    dar   daR
    comer   comeR
    ir   iR

And, of course, many other infinitives.

The R also appears in one place where you would not expect it: before consonants. Remember that in Spanish only the single flap r, not the multiple trill rr, is normally heard before consonants. Once again this new patterning will bear particular watching in cognate words.

Spanish	Portuguese
cuarto	quaRto
carne	caRne
tercero	teRceiro
porque	poRque
barba	baRba
Carlos	CaRlos

2. Spanish l / Portuguese l or L

You can safely use the Spanish l sound in Portuguese <u>except</u> at the end of syllables. In that location you will need to change to a kind of l sound that is similar to the l sound often said by English speakers in words like <u>fool</u>, <u>milk</u>. (It may sound to you like a u or a w.) We will indicate this sound with the symbol L. Repeat after your instructor and be alert to it in cognate words. Check below and in Part IV, exercise 12.

FROM SPANISH TO PORTUGUESE

papeL	maL	aLguma
hoteL	miL	faLta
iguaL	espanhoL	úLtimo
taL	soLteiro	deLgado

3. Spanish ll / Portuguese lh.

If your Spanish ll is the variety that has a definite l coloring to it, i.e. the kind that might be shown phonetically as ly, you can safely carry it over into Portuguese. If it is the kind that resembles a strong English y sound, or if it is the 'Argentinian' type ll, you cannot carry it over.

Obvious cognates:
milha
toalha
bilhete
falhar

Less obvious cognates:
fôlha
coelho
olhar
velho

4. Spanish ñ / Portuguese nh

Although the Portuguese nh may be considered the counterpart of Spanish ñ, the two sounds are not quite so similar as they may first appear to be. Let us compare Spanish leño with Portuguese lenho. In the Spanish word you can feel your tongue making contact with the roof of the mouth, just behind the upper front teeth. In the Portuguese word the tongue approaches this position, but drops away without making contact. The result is something which may sound to you like a nasalized y sound. As usual, your best approach is to carefully imitate a native model.

lenho   venho
unha   senhor
tenho   senhora

FROM SPANISH TO PORTUGUESE

Portuguese Consonants Not Occurring in Spanish

1. (**š**) - We are using this symbol to represent a sound which is not brand new to you since it occurs in English. It is very similar to the **sh** of 'shape'. It has several spellings.

   Examples: **ch**ega
   a**ch**o
   cai**x**a

2. (**ž**) - This symbol also stands for a sound that resembles an English sound. It is close to the **z** of 'azure'.

   Examples: **j**antar
   a**g**ência
   João

3. (**v**) - Whether or not a real **v** sound exists in Spanish (in most dialects it does not), it certainly does exist in Portuguese. It often occurs where you have been used to saying a **b** ('hard') or a ƀ ('soft') in Spanish. Check the cognates below. Also see exercise 9, Part IV, for additional practice.

Spanish	(Spelling altered when necessary to show **b** or ƀ sound)	Portuguese
barrer		varrer
bamos		vamos
bisitar		visitar
biƀir		viver
bista		vista
liƀro		livro
haƀer		haver
palaƀra		palavra
deƀer		dever

FROM SPANISH TO PORTUGUESE

plus Past II (Imperfect) forms
of regular -ar verbs:

tomaba	tomava
fumábamos	fumávamos
almorzaban	almoçavam
etc.	etc.

4. (z) - Though this sound may be heard occasionally in Spanish, it is not considered by most laymen to be a Spanish sound. It is very much a Portuguese sound, however, and you will need to get used to using it. It is frequently found between vowels and at the beginning of words. This may be particularly annoying when the words are cognates whose Spanish counterparts have an s sound in the same location.

Spanish (s sound)	Portuguese (z sound)
(Between vowels)	
casa	casa
mesa	mesa
azul	azul
preciso	preciso
riqueza	riqueza
(Beginning of word)	
cero	zero
zona	zona

The z sound also appears between vowels when the second vowel begins the next word, as in /somos americanos/. For additional practice with the z sound, see Part IV, exercise 11.

FROM SPANISH TO PORTUGUESE

Observations on Major Brazilian Dialect Differences

1. For many speakers, particularly in the Rio area, a d before an i sound is modified to sound much like the English j of 'judge'. Note that the i sound is often represented in spelling by the letter e.

   Examples: onde
              de nada
              dia
              disco

2. Likewise, for most of these same speakers a t before an i sound is modified to sound much like an English or Spanish ch.

   Examples: noite
              leite
              tia
              tinha

Consonant Clusters

The only combinations of Portuguese consonants that will be ne to you are initial pn and ps. They do not occur in Spanish, and th are not very common in Portuguese either. You will find them in just a few items like pneu (tire) and psicologia (psychology), and several related words. These clusters may sound strange at first, but they are not particularly difficult to master.

   Examples: pneu   psicologia
              pneumonia   psicólogo
                              psiquiatria

PART II

THE GRAMMAR

Introduction

You will find that you can carry much of your Spanish grammar into Portuguese. For example, nearly all of the major Portuguese verb tenses are close copies of something you already know in Spanish. The present tense, the two past tenses (Past I and II, or 'preterite' and 'imperfect', if you prefer), the present and past subjunctives, the conditional, the future, the commands, and most of the compound tenses all look and sound very much like they do in Spanish. And, more importantly, they usually behave that way too. Thus, for example, if you have already won the battle of the distribution of the two past tenses in Spanish, you will not need to re-fight it in Portuguese. The rules that guided you in the former are equally applicable in the latter. Likewise, if you have learned to use the Spanish present tense as a substitute for the future tense at those times when the future is rather imminent (e.g. lo veo mañana), you should have no problem doing the same thing in Portuguese. Verbs make up a large part of the grammar of both languages, and the high incidence of direct transfer from one to another will undoubtedly prove to be a most useful tool.

There are other areas where Portuguese is a near mirror-image of Spanish. Portuguese has the same rigid gender and number relationships between nouns and adjectives. The object pronoun system is at times conveniently similar, at other times surprisingly different. (More about this later.) Most conjunctions, prepositions and other relator-type words and expressions tend

FROM SPANISH TO PORTUGUESE

to operate as they do in Spanish. And so on. We could add other areas of similarity, but you will soon discover them for yourself as you progress through your course.

From what has just been said it would be easy for you to assum that _all_ of Portuguese is put together like Spanish. But at the same time you are sophisticated enough to suspect that this is not likely to be the case, and you are right. That is precisely what this section on grammar is all about. There are a number of areas where Portuguese does _not_ structure itself like Spanish. Sometimes the differences are major, sometimes they are minor, but always they loom as potential trouble spots for those who know Spanish. On the following pages we will concentrate on the most significant of these.

FROM SPANISH TO PORTUGUESE

Word Order

Word Order in Questions with Interrogative Words.

Notice the position of the verb and subject (actor) in the following sentences.

Spanish	Portuguese
1. ¿Cuándo va María?	Quando Maria vai? (or: Quando vai Maria?)
2. ¿Dónde está Pablo?	Onde Paulo está? (or: Onde está Paulo?)
3. ¿A qué hora sale el tren?	A que horas o trem sai? (or: A que horas sai o trem?)
4. ¿Cuánto gana él?	Quanto êle ganha? (or: Quanto ganha êle?)
5. ¿Cómo está su esposa?	Como a sua espôsa está? (or: Como está a sua espôsa?)

In questions beginning with interrogative words, where the interrogative word itself is not the subject (actor) of the sentence, most Spanish speakers will place the actor _after_ the verb. In contrast, Portuguese speakers will most likely place the actor before the verb, though in many instances, as we have indicated, the reverse pattern may also be heard. In both languages, if the interrogative word is itself the subject of the sentence, it can only precede the verb.

6. ¿Quién sabe?	Quem sabe?
7. ¿Qué pasó?	O que passou?

FROM SPANISH TO PORTUGUESE

Word Order in 'Yes-No' Questions

Now observe the order of actor and verb in these sentences.

	Spanish	Portuguese
1.	¿Habla ella inglés? (or)	
	¿Ella habla inglés?	Ela fala inglês?
2.	¿Ganó usted mucho? (or)	
	¿Usted ganó mucho?	O senhor ganhou muito?
3.	¿Está Teresa aquí? (or)	
	¿Teresa está aquí?	Teresa está aqui?
4.	¿Trabajan María y Olga en Rio? (or)	
	¿María y Olga trabajan en Rio?	Maria e Olga trabalham no Rio?

As a Spanish speaker you are free to place the actor either before or after the verb in 'yes-no' questions (those that can be answered 'yes' or 'no'). In Portuguese you have no such choice. You must use the 'actor + verb' sequence.

Word Order in Answers to 'Yes-No' Questions.

	Spanish	Portuguese
1.	¿Trajo su auto?	Trouxe o seu carro?
	Sí, lo traje.	Trouxe sim.
2.	¿Tiene un fósforo?	O senhor tem um fósforo?
	Sí, sí tengo.	Tenho sim.
3.	¿Es usted americano?	O senhor é americano?
	Sí, soy.	Sou sim.

FROM SPANISH TO PORTUGUESE

4. ¿Alquilaron ellos la casa?   Êles alugaram a casa?
   Sí, la alquilaron.   Alugaram sim.

5. ¿Conoce usted a los Molina? O senhor conhece os Molina?
   Sí, los conozco.   Conheço.

6. ¿Están con prisa?   Estão com pressa?
   Sí, están.   Estão.

Examples 1 through 4 above illustrate the positioning of the affirmative answer 'yes' with regard to the verb. In Spanish it is most likely to appear before the verb, separated from it by a pause. In Portuguese its most normal position is after the verb, with little, if any, pause separating the two.

Examples 5 and 6 illustrate a common variant of the Portuguese pattern: the omission of the 'yes'. This is possible in Spanish too, of course, but it is much less frequent than in Portuguese.

Negation

Basically, the process of making a verb or an entire utterance negative is the same in Portuguese as it is in Spanish. However, you should be aware of the following rather unique features.

An 'extra' negative

Portuguese sometimes adds a seemingly redundant negative (the word não) to the end of an utterance. The effect is to mildly emphasize the negative thought already expressed in the sentence.

    a. Não, não falei não.   'No, I didn't say (anything).'
    b. Não, não tem não.   'No, he doesn't have (it).'
    c. Não, não faça isso, não.   'No, don't do that.'

More likely than not, sentences a and b would be said in response to 'yes-no' questions.

Portuguese 'either / neither'

The sense of the Spanish negative tampoco is often rendered in Portuguese as também não, which always precedes the verb.

Spanish	Portuguese
a. Yo tampoco quiero.	Eu também não quero.
b. María no va tampoco.	Maria também não vai.
c. No me gusta tampoco.	Eu também não gosto.

Contractions

The only two contractions in Spanish are: de + el = del
                                             a + el = al

Portuguese has these two (in a somewhat different shape, to be sure) plus quite a few more. All of them involve combinations of the prepositions _em_, _de_, _a_ and _por_ with definite articles, demonstratives, personal pronouns, and the words _aqui_ and _outro_. We have tabulated most of them below. An empty box indicates a combination which does not contract.

CHART A: Prepositions plus definite articles.

	o	os	a	as
em	no	nos	na	nas
de	do*	dos	da	das
a	ao*	aos	à	às
por	pelo	pelos	pela	pelas

*Cf. Spanish: de + el = del
                a + el = al

FROM SPANISH TO PORTUGUESE

CHART B: **Prepositions plus indefinite articles**

	um	uns	uma	umas
em	num	nuns	numa	numas
de	dum	duns	duma	dumas
a	---	----	----	-----
por	---	----	----	-----

CHART C: **Prepositions plus demonstratives**

	êste(s) esta(s)	êsse(s) essa(s)	aquêle(s) aquela(s)	isto, isso aquilo
em	neste(s) nesta(s)	nesse(s) nessa(s)	naquele(s) naquela(s)	nisto, nisso naquilo
de	dêste(s) desta(s)	dêsse(s) dessa(s)	daquele(s) daquela(s)	disto, disso daquilo
a	-------	-------	àquele(s) àquela(s)	àquilo
por	-------	-------	---------	------

CHART D: **Prepositions plus pronouns**

	êle	ela	êles	elas
em	nêle	nela	nêles	nelas
de	dêle	dela	dêles	delas

CHART E: **Prepositions plus certain adverbs and adjectives**

	aqui	ali	ai	outro(s) outra(s)
em	----	---	--	noutro(s) noutra(s)
de	daqui	dali	daí	--------

To show you more clearly what we are talking about, we have listed a few examples below. Compare the Portuguese with the Spanish equivalent.

From Chart A:

	Portuguese			Spanish
(em + o + livro)		=	no livro	en el libro
(de + os + senhores)		=	dos senhores	de los señores
(por + a + senhora)		=	pela senhora	por la señora

37

FROM SPANISH TO PORTUGUESE

From Chart B:

Portuguese		Spanish
(em + um + livro)	= num livro	en un libro
(de + uma + senhora)	= duma senhora	de una señora
(de + umas + senhoras)	= dumas senhoras	de unas señoras

From Chart C:

Portuguese		Spanish
(em + êste + livro)	= neste livro	en este libro
(de + aquela + senhora)	= daquela senhora	de aquella señora
(a + aquêles + senhores)	= àqueles senhores	a aquellos señores

From Chart D:

Portuguese		Spanish
(em + êle)	= nêle	en él
(de + ela)	= dela	de ella
(de + êles)	= dêles	de ellos

From Chart E:

Portuguese		Spanish
(em + outro + livro)	= noutro livro	en otro libro
(em + outras + cidades)	= noutras cidades	en otras ciudades
(de + aqui)	= daqui	de aquí

Learning to use these contractions will be one of your most difficult challenges in learning Portuguese.

FROM SPANISH TO PORTUGUESE

Verbs

Verb Types

Portuguese and Spanish both have -<u>ar</u>, -<u>er</u> and -<u>ir</u> type verbs. In addition, Portuguese has a fourth type, -<u>or</u>, which is represented only by the irregular verb pôr (cf. Spanish poner) and its related compounds. Most Portuguese cognates are of the same type as their Spanish counterparts. However, watch out for the following common verbs which are -<u>ir</u> type in Spanish but -<u>er</u> type in Portuguese.

Spanish	Portuguese
vivir	viver
escribir	escrever
batir	bater
recibir	receber
sufrir	sofrer
ocurrir	ocorrer
gemir	gemer
hervir	ferver
morir	morrer

Regular Verb Forms

Portuguese regular verb forms are remarkably similar to Spanish regular verb forms. The chart below enables you to make a direct comparison of the major tense forms of three regular verbs: mandar, comer and abrir.[1] Do not be misled by exact duplication of spelling. Although some Portuguese and Spanish forms are spelled exactly alike, their pronunciation is always distinctively different.

---

[1] In both languages abrir is regular in all forms except the Past Participle: Spanish abierto / Portuguese aberto.

FROM SPANISH TO PORTUGUESE

		Spanish		Portuguese
Present Tense	yo	mando como abro	eu	mando como abro
	él	manda come abre	êle	manda come abre
	nosotros	mandamos comemos abrimos	nós	mandamos comemos abrimos
	ellos	mandan comen abren	êles	mandam comem abrem

		Spanish		Portuguese
Imperfect Tense	yo	mandaba comía abría	eu	mandava comia abria
	él	mandaba comía abría	êle	mandava comia abria
	nosotros	mandábamos comíamos abríamos	nós	mandávamos comíamos abríamos
	ellos	mandaban comían abrían	êles	mandavam comiam abriam

FROM SPANISH TO PORTUGUESE

Preterite Tense	yo	mandé comí abrí	eu	mandei comi abri	
	él	mandó comió abrió	êle	mandou comeu abriu	
	nosotros	mandamos comimos abrimos	nós	mandamos *comemos abrimos	
	ellos	mandaron comieron abrieron	êles	mandaram comeram abriram	
Future Tense	yo	mandaré comeré abriré	eu	mandarei comerei abrirei	
	él	mandará comerá abrirá	êle	mandará comerá abrirá	
	nosotros	mandaremos comeremos abriremos	nós	mandaremos comeremos abriremos	
	ellos	mandarán comerán abrirán	êles	mandarão comerão abrirão	

*This form is particularly difficult for a Spanish speaker to remember since he associates it with the present tense.

FROM SPANISH TO PORTUGUESE

Conditional Tense	yo	mandaría comería abriría	eu	mandaria comeria abriria
	él	mandaría comería abriría	êle	mandaria comeria abriria
	nosotros	mandaríamos comeríamos abriríamos	nós	mandaríamos comeríamos abriríamos
	ellos	mandarían comerían abrirían	êles	mandariam comeriam abririam
Present Subjunctive and Command Form	yo	mande coma abra	eu	mande coma abra
	él	mande coma abra	êle	mande coma abra
	nosotros	mandemos comamos abramos	nós	mandemos comamos abramos
	ellos	manden coman abran	êles	mandem comam abram

FROM SPANISH TO PORTUGUESE

	yo	mandara/-se comiera/-se abriera/-se - - - -	eu	mandasse comesse abrisse - - - -
	él	mandara/-se comiera/-se abriera/-se	êle	mandasse comesse abrisse
Past Subjunctive (Compare the Portuguese forms par- ticularly with the Spanish-<u>se</u> forms.)	nosotros	- - - - mandáramos/-semos comiéramos/-semos abriéramos/-semos - - - -	nós	- - - - mandássemos comêssemos abríssemos - - - -
	ellos	mandaran/-sen comieran/-sen abrieran/-sen	êles	mandassem comessem abrissem

Gerund	mandando comiendo abriendo	mandando *comendo *abrindo

Past Participle	mandado comido **dirigido	mandado comido **dirigido

*Notice the absence of diphthongs.
**The Past Participle of <u>abrir</u> cannot be used here since it is irregular.

FROM SPANISH TO PORTUGUESE

Irregular Verb Forms

Portuguese, like Spanish, has its fair share of irregular verbs in all tenses. You will quickly note that at times the irregularities are very similar to those in Spanish, and that at times they are quite different. For the most part, there is no easy way to categorize or compare these cross-language correspondences, or the lack of them. There are too many of them, and they are too varied and unpredictable. For instance, when you discover that 'I say' is digo, which is the same as the Spanish irregular form, you might analogize and guess that 'I do' as faqo. But your guess would be wrong. The word is faço, which is irregular, but in another way. And you know this only by learning it. In most instances you are better off approaching Portuguese irregular forms without reference to Spanish irregular forms.

We must point out, however, two wide-ranging patterns of irregularity that frequently have correspondences in Spanish. In many verbs, Portuguese closed o and closed e change to open O and open E, respectively, in stressed syllables of present tense forms. In cognate verbs these changes correspond respectively to the Spanish o to ue and e to ie changes. (The changes take place in a number of non-cognates as well.) We are listing below some of the more common cognates. In some cases other irregularities are also present.

Portuguese	Spanish
querer	querer
quEro, quEr(em)	quiero, quiere(n)
poder	poder
pOsso, pOde(m)	puedo, puede(n)

FROM SPANISH TO PORTUGUESE

pr**o**var	pr**o**bar
pr**O**vo, pr**O**va(m)	pr**ue**bo, pr**ue**ba(n)
alm**o**çar	alm**o**rzar
alm**O**ço, alm**O**ça(m)	alm**ue**rzo, alm**ue**rza(n)
m**o**strar	m**o**strar
m**O**stro, m**O**stra(m)	m**ue**stro, m**ue**stra(n)
n**e**gar	n**e**gar
n**E**go, n**E**ga(m)	n**ie**go, n**ie**ga(n)
com**e**çar	com**e**nzar
com**E**ço, com**E**ça(m)	com**ie**nzo, com**ie**nza(n)
n**e**var	n**e**var
n**E**va	n**ie**va
ch**o**ver	ll**o**ver
ch**O**ve	ll**ue**ve

(In -**ir** verbs, these correspondences are observable only in 3rd person forms.)

pref**e**rir	pref**e**rir
pref**E**re(m)	pref**ie**re(n)
div**e**rtir	div**e**rtir
div**E**rte(m)	div**ie**rte(n)
d**o**rmir	d**o**rmir
d**O**rme(m)	d**ue**rme(n)

Notice below, however, that in verbs where the Spanish vowel-to-diphthong change is followed by an **n** in the same syllable, the Portuguese cognate is likely to have a nasal vowel instead of an open **O** or **E**. (**Começar** in the above list is an exception.) The verbs that follow are irregular in Spanish. Only **sentir** and **mentir** are irregular in Portuguese. (The irregularity is the nasal **I** in the 1st person singular.)

45

FROM SPANISH TO PORTUGUESE

cotar	contar
coto, cota(m)	cuento, cuenta(n)
encotrar	encontrar
encotro, encotra(m)	encuentro, encuentra(n)
setir	sentir
sito, sete(m)	siento, siente(n)
setar	sentar
seto, seta(m)	siento, sienta(n)
pesar	pensar
peso, pesa(m)	pienso, piensa(n)
metir	mentir
mito, mete(m)	miento, miente(n)

Verb Constructions

In this section we examine several Portuguese verb constructions which differ slightly from their Spanish counterparts.

1. Spanish (ir + a + infinitive) vs. Portuguese (ir + infinitive)

    Spanish inserts an a between a form of the verb ir and a following infinitive. Portuguese does not. Observe these examples:

Spanish	Portuguese
voy a comer	vou comer
van a estudiar	vão estudar
iba a llegar	ia chegar
fueron a nadar	foram nadar

46

FROM SPANISH TO PORTUGUESE

2. Spanish (<u>haber</u> + past participle) vs. Portuguese (<u>ter</u> + past participle)

Spanish combines the verb <u>haber</u> with the -<u>do</u> form (the past participle) of the main verb to form a series of tenses which are traditionally called the 'perfect' tenses. We are referring to such items as:

> he comido
> habrá salido
> habían escrito
> habíamos trabajado
> si hubiera hecho

Portuguese has this kind of construction too, but it uses the verb <u>ter</u> (cognate with Spanish <u>tener</u>) instead of <u>haver</u>. The Portuguese constructions are parallel to the Spanish constructions <u>most</u> of the way. For example, we can say that the following, under most circumstances, are equivalents.

Spanish	Portuguese	English
habían escrito	tinham escrito	they had written
habríamos escrito	teríamos escrito	we would have written
habrán escrito	terão escrito	they will have written
si hubiera escrito	se tivesse escrito	if I had written

Now, however, we come to a slight, but very important, exception. The present tense of Spanish <u>haber</u> + verb is usually <u>not</u> the exact equivalent of the present tense of Portuguese <u>ter</u> + verb. Observe carefully:

<u>Spanish</u>:	he escrito	I have written
<u>Portuguese</u>:	tenho escrito	I have <u>been</u> <u>writing</u>
<u>Spanish</u>:	hemos trabajado	We have worked
<u>Portuguese</u>:	temos trabalhado	We have <u>been</u> <u>working</u>

47

FROM SPANISH TO PORTUGUESE

The Portuguese construction shows a kind of progression of action from some point in the past, up to and into the prese This is indicated in the English translation been + ...ing. To express the equivalent of the above Spanish examples, Portuguese would use the simple past I (preterite) tense. Thus:

Spanish	Portuguese
he escrito	escrevi
hemos trabajado	trabalhamos

3. Spanish gustar vs. Portuguese gostar (de)

As you know, in Spanish if you want to express the idea th you like a certain thing you have to turn the thought arou and say that that thing is pleasing to you. But you do no do this in Portuguese. You simply say that you like it, j as you do in English. The item in question is not conceiv of, grammatically, as being 'pleasing to you', which is th case in Spanish. Compare these examples. (Notice that th preposition de must follow gostar.)

Spanish	Portuguese
Me gusta el libro.	Eu gosto do livro.
Me gustan esas chicas.	Eu gosto dessas meninas.
Nos gusta viajar.	Nós gostamos de viajar.
Les gusta estudiar.	Êles gostam de estudar.

4. Spanish hacer vs. Portuguese haver in time expressions.

Spanish	Portuguese
1. a. Hace dos años que trabajo aquí.	Há dois anos que trabalho aqui.
b. Trabajo aquí desde hace dos años.	Trabalho aqui há dois anos.

FROM SPANISH TO PORTUGUESE

2. a. **Hace** dos meses que llegué.   **Há** dois meses que cheguei.
   b. Llegué **hace** dos meses.   Cheguei **há** dois meses.

The patterning in these Portuguese utterances pretty closely parallels the patterning in the Spanish. The difference is in the use of a form of **haver** (cf. Spanish **haber**) in a slot where you are accustomed to using a form of **hacer**. Portuguese speakers can also use **faz**, from **fazer**, in these utterances, but **há** seems to be preferred by most.

[European Portuguese only: Spanish **estar** + **-ndo** vs. Portuguese **estar** + **a** + infinitive.]

Spanish	Portuguese
El presidente **está hablando**.	O presidente **está a falar**.
Estoy leyendo.	**Estou a ler**.
Estaban almorzando.	**Estavam a almoçar**.

Although European Portuguese uses the **estar** + **-ndo** construction on occasion, the **estar** + **a** + infinitive construction is more common.

Usage of Ser and Estar

The distribution of **ser** and **estar** in Portuguese is very nearly the same as it is in Spanish. Observe these instances of identical usage.

Origin:	**Es** de México.	**É** do México.
Time:	**Son** las tres.	**São** três.
Possession:	**Son** míos.	**São** meus.
Nouns:	**Es** médico.	**É** médico.
Characteristics:	**Son** bonitas.	**São** bonitas.
Passive voice:	La carta **fue** escrita hoy.	A carta **foi** escrita hoje.

49

FROM SPANISH TO PORTUGUESE

Conditions: El carro **está** sucio.   O carro **está** sujo.
La carta **está** escrita.   A carta **está** escrita.

There is just one important area where there is a significan difference in the distribution of these two verbs in the two languages - the area at times referred to, perhaps rather loosely, as 'location'. You will remember that Spanish uses the verb **está** to state the location or position of a person or thing.

Juan **está** en California.
California **está** en los Estados Unidos.
Los niños **están** en el centro.
El banco **está** en el centro.

In speaking Portuguese you will need to decide whether the location is fixed or transitory. If it is fixed, i.e. geographically fixed, **ser** will be your choice.

A California **é** nos Estados Unidos.
O banco **é** no centro.

If it is not geographically fixed, but transitory or temporary in nature, **estar** will be your choice.

Os meninos **estão** no centro.
João **está** na California.

Portuguese frequently uses the verb **ficar** in place of **ser** to indicate fixed location. This is analogous to the Spanish verb **quedar** (not **quedarse**) substituting for **estar** under the same circumstances.

<u>Spanish</u>   <u>Portuguese</u>
El hotel **está** en la calle quince.   O hotel **é** na rua quinze.
              or   or
El hotel **queda** en la calle quince. O hotel **fica** na rua quinze.

50

FROM SPANISH TO PORTUGUESE

¿Dónde **está** Santo Domingo? Onde **é** São Domingos?

   or   or

¿Dónde **queda** Santo Domingo? Onde **fica** São Domingos?

Two New Verb Categories

1. Future subjunctive.

One of the major differences between Portuguese grammar and Spanish grammar is the fact that Portuguese has a very active future subjunctive, whereas Spanish does not. As you know, the future subjunctive is quite rare in conversational Spanish, being reserved, for the most part, for rather formal and literary speech This is not so in Portuguese. The Portuguese future subjunctive is an everyday occurrence in the speech of nearly every native speaker of the language.

You will soon see that in many instances Portuguese uses a future subjunctive where Spanish uses a **present** subjunctive. For example, Portuguese calls for a future subjunctive after such conjunctions as **quando, logo que, assim que, depois que, se,** and others, when the reference is to future time. Spanish would normally use a present subjunctive after the Spanish equivalent of these conjunctions (except after **si,** of course) when the reference is to future time. Compare these examples.

	Spanish (present subjunctive)	Portuguese (future subjunctive)
1.	Cuando yo **vaya**, voy por avión.	Quando eu **fôr**, vou de avião.
2.	Tan pronto como **sepamos**, se lo decimos.	Logo que **soubermos**, lhe dizemos.

FROM SPANISH TO PORTUGUESE

3. Pienso almorzar después
que ellos salgan.

   Penso almoçar depois que
êles saírem.

4. Voy a decirle cuando
llegue.

   Vou dizer-lhe quando
chegar.

5. Mientras ellos estén allí,
no voy.

   Enquanto êles estiverem
lá, não vou.

After the word 'if', when the reference is to the future, Portuguese again uses the future subjunctive. Spanish, you recall, cannot use a present subjunctive under such circumstances. Normally, a simple present tense would be used.

Spanish	Portuguese

1. Si él viene, vamos a comer juntos.

   Se êle vier, vamos comer juntos.

2. Voy si es posible.

   Vou se fôr possível.

3. Si usted no puede, avíseme.

   Se o senhor não puder, avise-me.

2. Personal infinitive

We come now to another major structural difference. Portuguese can 'personalize' an infinitive by attaching certain 'actor-markers' or endings, to it. Spanish does not do this.

The 'actor-markers' that Portuguese uses are the first and third plural endings -mos and -em. There are no endings for the singular. A sample verb paradigm would look like this:

	Singular	Plural
1st	chegar	chegarmos
2nd, 3rd	chegar	chegarem

The problem, as usual, is not so much learning the forms as it is when to use them. As a Spanish speaker you will have to deal with conflicts that the Portuguese personal infinitive sets up with some of your Spanish subjunctive patterns. In other words, the personal infinitive is very often used in Portuguese where a subjunctive would be normal in Spanish. This is observable when the verb in question follows after:

a. an impersonal expression
b. the verbs 'to tell' and 'to ask'
c. certain Spanish conjunctions (clause relators) which may convert to prepositions in Portuguese.

Let us examine each of these three categories separately.

a) After impersonal expressions

Spanish (subjunctive)	Portuguese (personal infinitive)
1. Es mejor que **hagamos** eso ahora.	É melhor **fazermos** isso agora.
2. Es difícil que **salgamos** temprano.	É difícil **sairmos** cedo.
3. Es natural que **hablen** inglés.	É natural **falarem** inglés.
4. Es posible que yo no **venga**.	É possível eu não **vir**.[1]
5. Es preciso que **estudien**.	É preciso (êles) **estudarem**.
6. Es peor que **haga** eso.	É pior (êle) **fazer** isso.[1]
7. No conviene que **paguen** ahora.	Não é conveniente êles **pagarem** agora.

---

[1]Notice there is no ending on these singular forms.

FROM SPANISH TO PORTUGUESE

Portuguese could also use a present subjunctive to express most of the above ideas, just as Spanish does. Thus rephrased, the first several utterances would be:

É melhor que <u>façamos</u> isso agora.
É difícil que <u>saiamos</u> cedo.
É natural que <u>falem</u> inglês.
É possível que eu não <u>venha</u>.

There may or may not be a slight tendency to prefer the personal infinitive over the subjunctive in cases like these where there is a choice. To prepare yourself for any eventuality, we suggest that you learn to recognize and handle both patterns.

b) After 'to tell' and 'to request'

	Spanish (subjunctive)	Portuguese (personal infinitive)
1.	Yo pedí que ellos se <u>quedaran</u>.	Eu pedi para <u>ficarem</u>.
2.	Juan pide que <u>ayudemos</u>.	João pede para <u>ajudarmos</u>.
3.	Dígales a las niñas que <u>pongan</u> la mesa.	Diga para as meninas <u>porem</u> a mesa.
4.	Nos dijeron que <u>saliéramos</u>.	Êles nos disseram para <u>sairmos</u>.

When the verb in the main clause is 'to tell' or 'to request', Spanish puts the verb in the other (subordinate) clause in the subjunctive. Portuguese is very likely to use the personal infinitive, although, once again, the subjunctive is common. (Eu pedi que êles <u>ficassem</u>.), etc. As before, we suggest you learn both patterns.

Notice that <u>para</u> is used to link the two clauses.

FROM SPANISH TO PORTUGUESE

c) After certain Spanish conjunctions (or clause relators) which may convert to prepositions in Portuguese.

Spanish (subjunctive)	Portuguese (personal infinitive)
1. Llegué __sin que__ me __vieran__.	Cheguei __sem__ êles me __verem__.
2. Vamos a trabajar __hasta que__ ellos __lleguen__.	Vamos trabalhar __até__ êles __chegarem__.
3. Tengo que quedarme aquí __hasta que estén__ listos todos.	Tenho que ficar aqui __até__ todos __estarem__ prontos.
4. Van a salir __antes de que__ los __conozcamos__.	Vão sair __antes de__ os __conhecermos__.
5. Explica todo __para que__ ellos __comprendan__.	Explica tudo __para__ êles __compreenderem__.

Spanish must use a subjunctive to express the above ideas. Portuguese seems to prefer the personal infinitive, but will often do as Spanish does and use a conjunction followed by subjunctive.

For example: Cheguei sem que êles me __vissem__.
Vamos trabalhar até que êles __cheguem__.

Once again, we recommend that you learn both patterns.

Another area of conflict for you involves the Portuguese personal infinitive and the Spanish infinitive. After prepositions, Portuguese frequently uses the personal infinitive. Spanish uses just the infinitive.

Spanish (infinitive)	Portuguese (personal infinitive)
1. Después de __comer__, vamos a mirar la televisión.	Depois de __comermos__, vamos olhar televisão.

55

2. Al <u>salir</u> de aquí, vamos Ao <u>sairmos</u> daqui, vamos
   a casa.   a casa.

3. Ellas van a poner la mesa   Elas vão pôr a mesa antes
   antes de <u>irse</u>.   de <u>irem</u>.

4. Por <u>haber</u> trabajado tanto,   Por <u>terem</u> trabalhado tanto,
   están muy cansados.   estão muito cansados.

FROM SPANISH TO PORTUGUESE

Nominals

Object Pronouns

1. Placement

Your most formidable task in mastering the object pronouns will be learning where to put them. In Spanish, the arrangement of verb and object pronouns (direct, indirect and reflexive) is a rather complex affair. In Portuguese it may seem even more so, largely because of interference from Spanish. Let us check on some specific cases.

A. Object pronouns with a conjugated verb form

Spanish	Portuguese
1. Ana se sienta.	Ana se senta.
	Ana senta-se.
2. Ella me conoce.	Ela me conhece.
	Ela conhece-me.
3. Pablo le dio un dólar.	Paulo lhe deu um dólar.
	Paulo deu-lhe um dólar.

In utterances like those above, in which a noun or personal pronoun precedes the conjugated verb, Spanish must put the object pronoun **before** the conjugated verb form. Portuguese may put it **before** or **after**, with a preference, in Brazilian Portuguese, for putting it **before**.

Now, notice these examples:

Spanish	Portuguese
4. Me levanté temprano.	Levantei-me cedo.
5. Me conoce bien.	Conhece-me bom.
6. Le dio un dólar.	Deu-lhe um dólar.

57

FROM SPANISH TO PORTUGUESE

No noun or pronoun precedes the conjugated verb in these examples. Spanish speakers, as always, must let the object pronoun _precede_ the verb. Most Portuguese speakers, however, avoid beginning an utterance with an object pronoun, preferring instead to place it _after_ the verb, as shown above.

Now, here are still more examples:

Spanish	Portuguese
7. No se levanta.	Não se levanta.
8. No me conoce.	Não me conhece.
9. ¿Quién le dio un dólar?	Quem lhe deu um dólar?

The rule in effect for these Portuguese sentences is that if anything other than a noun or personal pronoun subject precedes the verb, the object pronoun is placed _before_ the verb. These sentences and others like them fall right into the familiar Spanish pattern, so in themselves they represent nothing strikingly new to you. (However, compare them with examples 1, 2, and 3 above, where the verb is preceded by a noun, and the object pronoun may therefore either go before that verb _or_ _follow_ _after_ _it_.)

B. Object pronouns with an infinitive

Spanish	Portuguese
1. Juan va a levantar**se**.	João vai levantar-**se**.
Juan **se** va a levantar.	João vai **se** levantar.
2. Juan quiere llevar**me** al centro.	João quer levar-**me** ao centro.
Juan **me** quiere llevar al centro.	João **me** quer levar ao centro.
3. Juan puede decir**me** eso.	João pode dizer-**me** isso.
Juan **me** puede decir eso.	João **me** pode dizer isso.
4. ... para recibir**nos**.	... para receber-**nos**.
	... para **nos** receber.

FROM SPANISH TO PORTUGUESE

In verbal constructions containing an infinitive and an auxiliary verb, Spanish puts object pronouns either after the infinitive or before the auxiliary.

In the same constructions, Portuguese puts object pronouns either after the infinitive (like Spanish) or before the infinitive (quite unlike Spanish).

C. Object pronouns with the present participle (the -ndo form)

Spanish	Portuguese
1. Juan está levantándose.	João está levantando-se.
Juan se está levantando.	João está se levantando.
2. Juan está llevándome.	João está levando-me.
Juan me está llevando.	João está me levando.
3. Juan está diciéndole.	João está dizendo-lhe.
Juan le está diciendo.	João está lhe dizendo.

The situation with the -ndo forms is similar to that which we have described for the infinitives. In Spanish the object pronoun may go after the participle or before the auxiliary verb. In Portuguese it may go after the participle (which is done in Spanish), or before the participle (which is never done in Spanish).

FROM SPANISH TO PORTUGUESE

2. Other Problems.

In addition to handling the major problems of accurate placement, you will need to make other adjustments in order to control
the complex of object pronouns in Portuguese.

A. Modification of infinitive and direct object pronoun.

Spanish	Portuguese
1. Pablo va a llevarla.	Paulo vai levá-la.
2. Ella va a mandarlos.	Ela vai mandá-los.
3. Ellos van a hacerlo.	Êles vão fazê-lo.

The Portuguese third person direct object pronouns o, os, a,
as change their forms to lo, los, la, las when they follow an
infinitive. As such they look and sound suspiciously like the
comparable Spanish forms. Be sure to notice that in this construction the infinitive loses its r. It is almost as if the
r changed to l.

B. Frequent omission of direct object pronoun in Portuguese

Spanish	Portuguese
1. ¿Quién compró los billetes?	Quem comprou os bilhetes?
Pablo los compró.	Paulo comprou.
2. Envuélvelo sin la caja.	Embrulhe sem a caixa.

FROM SPANISH TO PORTUGUESE

3. María lo vio.   Maria viu o senhor.
    (Mary saw you)   (Mary saw you)

4. Yo las llevo.   Eu levo as senhoras.
    (I'll take you)   (I'll take you)

Spanish needs the object pronoun in these utterances. Portuguese can do without it. When the direct object is inanimate (as in numbers 1 and 2) the pronoun is often just simply omitted. When the direct object is 'you' (as in numbers 3 and 4), o senhor, a senhora, etc. are usually used in preference to the object pronouns.

C. Substitution of (a / para) for indirect object pronouns

   Spanish   Portuguese

1. Ella le dio un   Ela lhe deu um presente.   (or)
   regalo.   Ela deu um presente a êle.   (or)
                             Ela deu um presente para êle.

2. El me contó una   Êle me contou uma história.   (or)
   historia.   Êle contou uma história a mim.   (or)
                             Êle contou uma história para mim.

3. Quiero decirle.   Quero dizer-lhe.   (or)
                             Quero dizer ao senhor.   (or)
                             Quero dizer para o senhor.

Portuguese speakers frequently use a prepositional phrase with a or para in place of the indirect object pronoun. Spanish can occasionally do this with para, with the meaning 'for', but can not ordinarily do it with a.

For example: Te tengo un regalito.
               Tengo un regalito para ti.

FROM SPANISH TO PORTUGUESE

Notice that the prepositional phrase in Portuguese is used in place of the object pronoun, and not as a redundant addition to it. Such redundancies are common in Spanish, but they do not occur in Portuguese.

Spanish	Portuguese	
1. A mí me parece.	Parece-me.	
2. Le doy esto a usted.	Dou-lhe isto.	(or)
	Dou isto ao senhor.	
3. Quiero decirle a Pablo...	Quero dizer-lhe...	(or)
	Quero dizer para Paulo...	

You will not say: Dou-lhe isto ao senhor, with both lhe and ao senhor.

D. **Spanish pronoun arrangements not appearing in Portuguese**

a. Indirect and direct object pronouns combined

Spanish	Portuguese	
1. Me lo dio. (the check)	Deu-me.	(or)
	Deu-me o cheque.	
2. Se la presté. (the pen)	Emprestei-lhe.	(or)
	Emprestei-lhe a caneta.	

In Spanish the combination of indirect and direct object pronoun in utterances like those above is very common. In Portuguese it may occur but is almost always avoided in everyday speech. Either the direct object pronoun is omitted, or the direct object noun is used in its stead.

FROM SPANISH TO PORTUGUESE

b. Reflexive and direct object pronouns combined

Spanish	Portuguese
1. Juan se lo comió. (the bread)	(Nothing comparable)
2. Me la tomé. (the milk)	(Nothing comparable)
3. Se las llevó Alicia. (the keys)	(Nothing comparable)

c. Reflexive and indirect object pronouns combined

Spanish	Portuguese
1. Se me olvidó la llave.	(Nothing comparable)
2. Se nos quedó en casa.	(Nothing comparable)
3. Se le cayeron unas tazas.	(Nothing comparable)

Direct Object Nouns

Spanish inserts a 'personal a' before a personalized, direct object noun. Portuguese does not have the 'personal a'.

Spanish	Portuguese
1. Veo a María.	Vejo Maria.
2. Conozco al presidente.	Conheço o presidente.

Definite Article

Portuguese may use the definite article along with the possessive pronoun. Spanish does not do this.

Spanish	Portuguese
mi amigo	o meu amigo
mis amigos	os meus amigos
mi amiga	a minha amiga
mis amigas	as minhas amigas

FROM SPANISH TO PORTUGUESE

Gender

1. Gender in cognates

In most cases, Portuguese cognates have the same gender as their Spanish counterparts. There are some common exceptions to this, however, and we will list some of them here.

A. Many Spanish masculine words ending in -aje are feminine in Portuguese and end in -agem.

For example:

Spanish	Portuguese
el viaje	a viagem
el paisaje	a paisagem
el masaje	a massagem
el mensaje	a mensagem
el sabotaje	a sabotagem

B. Others:

Spanish	Portuguese
el color	a côr
el dolor	a dor
el árbol	a árvore
el puente	a ponte
el partido 'game'	a partida
el equipo	a equipe
la nariz	o nariz
la leche	o leite
la sonrisa	o sorriso
la sal	o sal

2. Gender in the Number 'Two'.

Portuguese has gender agreement for the number 'two'. Spani does not. Remembering to make this agreement in Portuguese is no always as easy as it may seem.

Spanish	Portuguese
dos libros	dois livros
dos señoras	duas senhoras

FROM SPANISH TO PORTUGUESE

PART III
HINTS ON VOCABULARY TRANSFER

Much of your Portuguese vocabulary will come via direct transfer from Spanish. Vocabulary transfer has been implicit in our discussion of sounds in Part I. We showed there how certain correspondences can guide you in the process. We indicated, for example, the great utility of knowing that Spanish ie and ue often correspond to Portuguese E and O, respectively, and that Spanish -ión, -on and -an (the latter two both stressed and unstressed) often correspond to the Portuguese nasal diphthong -ãu. In this section we will examine other correspondences, many of them not involving new sounds. We have attempted to separate the common ones from those that occur only occasionally. We have reserved a special place for those that involve word endings.

As a final note on vocabulary transfer we have listed several items that can be transferred only with considerable caution: false cognates.

Some Patterns of Correspondences

Common Correspondences

1. Sounds

    The Spanish h sound does not exist in Portuguese. In cognate words the h sound usually converts to one of three sounds: š, ž or lh. Study these groupings:

    a. Spanish h   Portuguese š (sh of English 'ship')

        jefe   chefe
        bajo   baixo
        quejarse   queixar-se
        embajada   embaixada
        caja   caixa
        dejar   deixar
        bruja   bruxa

65

FROM SPANISH TO PORTUGUESE

b. Spanish **h**   Portuguese **j** (**z** of English 'azure')

    junio   junho
    julio   julho
    junto   junto
    juez   juiz
    generoso   generoso
    gente   gente
    joven   jovem
    ligera   ligeira
    jugar   jogar
    adjectivo   adjetivo
    sargento   sargento
    extranjero   estrangeiro
    jardín   jardim
    reloj   relógio
    viaje   viagem
    página   página

c. Spanish **h**   Portuguese **lh** (**ll** of Spanish 'calle')

    mujer   mulher
    orejas   orelhas
    mejor   melhor
    trabajar   trabalhar
    mojar   molhar
    escoger   escolher
    abeja   abelha
    viejo   velho
    ojo   ôlho
    aguja   agulha

NOTE: Spanish **jabón** / Portuguese **sabão** (**s** of English 'Sam')
Note also: Spanish **ejemplo, ejercicio** / Portuguese **exemplo, exercício** (where the **x** is pronounced like **z** of English 'zebra')

FROM SPANISH TO PORTUGUESE

Spanish **ll** sometimes shows up as **l**, sometimes as **ẓ**, and sometimes as **lh** (no change). Study these groupings:

a. **Spanish ll**   **Portuguese l**

    bello   belo
    cabello   cabelo
    llevar   levar
    gallina   galinha
    amarillo   amarelo
    ella   ela
    allí   ali
    villa   vila
    caballo   cavalo
    callar   calar
    fallecer   falecer

b. **Spanish ll**   **Portuguese ẓ**

    llorar   chorar
    llamar   chamar
    llegar   chegar
    llave   chave
    llover   chover
    llano   chão
    lleno   cheio

c. **Spanish ll**   **Portuguese lh**

    fallar   falhar
    milla   milha
    millón   milhão
    toalla   toalha
    billete   bilhete

Notice that Spanish **ll** appears between **vowels** in the first group (with the exception of **llevar**), and at the **beginning** of the words in the second group.

FROM SPANISH TO PORTUGUESE

Spanish n often corresponds to Portuguese nh; and conversely, Portuguese n often corresponds to Spanish ñ. Observe these groupings.

a)
Spanish n	Portuguese nh
dinero	dinheiro
camino	caminho
ganar	ganhar
sobrina	sobrinha
tocino	toucinho
vino	vinho
amanecer	amanhecer
cocina	cozinha
espina	espinha

b)
Spanish ñ	Portuguese n
año	ano
pequeño	pequeno
caña	cana
enseñar	ensinar
dañar	danar
pestaña	pestana

■ Portuguese inserts an f sound in a number of words where Spanish has the 'silent' printed h.

Spanish	Portuguese
higo	figo
hígado	fígado
hacer	fazer
hormiga	formiga
hacienda	fazenda
herir	ferir

FROM SPANISH TO PORTUGUESE

humo	fumo
hervir	ferver
hierro	ferro
hazaña	façanha
*hijo	filho
*hoja	fôlha
huracán	furacão
almohada	almofada

■ Spanish ch often corresponds to Portuguese t.

Spanish	Portuguese
aprovechar	aproveitar
techo	teto
noche	noite
leche	leite
luchar	lutar
estrecho	estreito
hecho	feito
ocho	oito
mucho	muito

■ Previously, in another context, we mentioned that sometimes the Spanish s sound corresponds to the Portuguese z sound. Let us review that point.

Spanish	Portuguese (z sound underlined)
casa	casa
cosa	coisa
blusa	blusa
música	música
acusar	acusar

*See grouping c. on page 66.)

FROM SPANISH TO PORTUGUESE

veces	vêzes
hacer	fazer
cocina	cozinha
azul	azul
zorro	zorro

■ Spanish kt is often reduced to just t in Portuguese

Spanish	Portuguese
acto	ato
doctor	doutor
dictador	ditador
actual	atual
contacto	contato
carácter	caráter
víctima	vítima
perfecto	perfeito
practicar	praticar
arquitectura	arquitetura

■ Many Spanish words containing ks lose the k in the Portuguese cognate.

Spanish	Portuguese
acción	ação
sección	seção
lección	lição
accidente	acidente
occidental	ocidental

There are exceptions. Note Portuguese ficção and succão, both of which retain the k sound.

■ Likewise, Spanish words containing mn are likely to lose the m in the Portuguese cognate.

Spanish	Portuguese
alumno	aluno
columna	coluna
himno	hino
solemne	solene
amnistía	anistia
indemnizar	indenizar
calumnia	calúnia

The m is retained in **amnésia**.

■ The l sound, as the second element of a Spanish cluster, often changes to an r sound in Portuguese. This happens quite frequently if the first element of the cluster is p, much less frequently in other cases.

Spanish	Portuguese
placer	prazer
playa	praia
plato	prato
plata	prata
plaza	praça
plaga	praga
plazo	prazo
cumplir	cumprir
emplear	empregar
sable	sabre
blanco	branco
doblar	dobrar
noble	nobre
obligar	obrigar

FROM SPANISH TO PORTUGUESE

```
flaco        fraco
flota        frota
iglesia      igreja
esclavo      escravo
```

- Spanish -ano often corresponds to Portuguese -ão.[1]

Spanish	Portuguese
mano	mão
hermano	irmão
verano	verão
anciano	ancião
sano	são
aldeano	aldeão

Notice, however, Portuguese puritano, and colombiano, americano, venezuelano, persiano and many other nationalities.

- Spanish -ana often corresponds to Portuguese -ã

Spanish	Portuguese
hermana	irmã
manzana	maçã
mañana	amanhã
alemana	alemã
anciana	anciã
aldeana	aldeã
sana	sã

Notice, however, Portuguese campana, puritana, banana, as well as americana, colombiana and many other nationalities.

---

[1] For other correspondences involving ão, see pages 18-19.

FROM SPANISH TO PORTUGUESE

2. Word Endings

■ Most Spanish adjectives ending in -**ble** will end in -**vel** in Portuguese.

Spanish	Portuguese
horrible	horrível
terrible	terrível
favorable	favorável
notable	notável
posible	possível
indispensable	indispensável
amable	amável
agradable	agradável

■ Portuguese equivalents of Spanish words ending in -**dad** (or -**tad**) and -**tud** usually add an unstressed **i** sound. In addition, the **t** of Spanish -**tad** is likely to be a **d** in Portuguese.

Spanish	Portuguese
verdad	verdade
dignidad	dignidade
facilidad	facilidade
dificultad	dificuldade
lealtad	lealdade
libertad	liberdade
magnitud	magnitude
actitud	atitude

Some of the more notable exceptions:

aptitud	aptidão
amistad	amizade

73

FROM SPANISH TO PORTUGUESE

- The s sound of the Spanish endings -eza and -oso corresponds to a z sound in Portuguese.

Spanish	Portuguese
firmeza	firmeza
riqueza	riqueza
gentileza	gentileza
fortaleza	fortaleza
poderoso	poderoso
famoso	famoso
amoroso	amoroso
espantoso	espantoso

- The Spanish diminutive endings -ito(a) and -cito(a) correspond to Portuguese -inho(a) and -zinho(a)

Spanish	Portuguese
carrito	carrinho
Pablito	Paulinho
mesita	mesinha
casita	casinha
cafecito	cafèzinho
pobrecita	pobrezinha

- The Spanish noun-ending -ero generally corresponds to the Portuguese noun-ending -eiro. Notice the diphthong in the Portuguese forms.

Spanish	Portuguese
portero	porteiro
cartero	carteiro
minero	mineiro

FROM SPANISH TO PORTUGUESE

zapatero   sapateiro
vaquero   vaqueiro
cocinero   cozinheiro

■ The Spanish words **presencia**, **diferencia**, **licencia** and **sentencia** lose the **ia** diphthong in Portuguese. Most other words ending in -**encia** retain it. Thus:

Spanish	Portuguese
presencia	presença
diferencia	diferença
licencia	licença
sentencia	sentença

but

eficiencia	eficiência
paciencia	paciência
inteligencia	inteligência
providencia	providência
esencia	essência
competencia	competência

[Other word endings already discussed in other contexts include Spanish -**ción** / Portuguese -**ção** (see page 19), and Spanish -**aje** / Portuguese -**agem** (see page 64).]

ess Common Correspondences

The correspondences listed below are found in a smaller umber of cognates than those listed above under 'Common Correspondences.' The cognates themselves may, of course, be very common words. In some cases, the examples given may be the only ones of their kind.

FROM SPANISH TO PORTUGUESE

■ Absence of l in Portuguese

Spanish	Portuguese
salir	sair
volar	voar
doler	doer
saludar	saudar
diablo	diabo

■ Absence of n in Portuguese

Spanish	Portuguese
comenzar	começar
moneda	moeda
defensa	defesa
venado	veado
amenaza	ameaça
luna	lua
crimen	crime

■ Absence of l or n and adjacent vowel in Portuguese.

Spanish	Portuguese
color	côr
dolor	dor
poner	pôr
tener	ter
venir	vir
general	geral
sólo	só
ganado	gado

FROM SPANISH TO PORTUGUESE

- Absence of *r* in Portuguese

Spanish	Portuguese
almorzar	almoçar
sangre	sangue
rostro	rosto

- Absence of *br* in Portuguese

Spanish	Portuguese
nombre	nome
hombre	homem
acostumbrarse	acostumar-se

- *n* becomes *l* in Portuguese

Spanish	Portuguese
naranja	laranja
berenjena	berinjela

- Reversal of vowel and consonant

Spanish	Portuguese
preguntar	perguntar
apretar	apertar

- Shift of diphthong, from after the consonant to **before** the consonant.

Spanish	Portuguese
apio	aipo
barrio	bairro
novio	noivo

FROM SPANISH TO PORTUGUESE

- Vowel changes

1. Spanish e to Portuguese i

Spanish	Portuguese
eso	isso
lengua	língua
venganza	vingança
edad	idade
profesional	profissional
enseñar	ensinar
corregir	corrigir
vecino	vizinho

2. Spanish u to Portuguese o

Spanish	Portuguese
jugar	jogar
ocurrir	ocorrer
sufrir	sofrer
rutina	rotina
cubrir	cobrir

3. Spanish o to Portuguese u

Spanish	Portuguese
costar	custar
sorpresa	surprêsa
sordo	surdo

FROM SPANISH TO PORTUGUESE

■ Spanish vowel to Portuguese diphthong

Spanish	Portuguese
casi	quase
más	mais
jamás	jamais
caja	caixa
bajo	baixo
dos	dois
cosa	coisa
noche	noite
poco	pouco
tesoro	tesouro

■ Spanish diphthong to Portuguese vowel

Spanish	Portuguese
cuaderno	caderno
antigua	antiga
treinta	trinta
veinte	vinte

■ Changes in stress patterns (Portuguese stress underlined.)

Spanish	Portuguese
policía	pol_í_cia
teléfono	telef_o_ne
límite	lim_i_te
nivel	n_í_vel

FROM SPANISH TO PORTUGUESE

False Cognates

Cognates are useful, but false or misleading ones are troublesome. Here are several to watch out for.

Spanish		Portuguese	
exquisito	(exquisite)	esquisito	(rare, unusual)
rubio	(blond)	ruivo	(red head)
rojo	(red)	roxo	(purple)
largo	(long)	largo	(wide)
rato	(while, time)	rato	(rat)
escoba	(broom)	escôva	(brush)
cena	(supper)	cena	(scene)
apellido	(family name)	apelido	(nickname)
sobrenombre	(nickname)	sobrenome	(family name)
cuarto	(room)	quarto	(bedroom)
cadera	(hip)	cadeira	(chair)
escritorio	(desk)	escritório	(office)
traer	(to bring)	trair	(to betray)
reparar	(to repare)	reparar	(to notice)
acordar(se)	(to remember)	acordar	(to awake)
barata	(cheap)	barata	(cockroach)

FROM SPANISH TO PORTUGUESE

PART IV

SUPPLEMENTARY PRONUNCIATION EXERCISES

The following exercises are provided on tape to give you additional help in keeping your pronunciation free of Spanish. They are keyed to the discussion of Portuguese sounds found in Part I. In order to avoid involvement with extraneous details and in order to permit maximum concentration on the point being drilled, very close cognates have been selected. All examples are Portuguese.

1. Portuguese weak-stressed ǝ sound (as underlined). (See Part I, pages 1-4.)

tom<u>a</u>	dig<u>a</u>
pas<u>sa</u>	com<u>a</u>
par<u>a</u>	abr<u>a</u>
pag<u>a</u>	beb<u>a</u>
visit<u>a</u>	sig<u>a</u>
mud<u>a</u>	respond<u>a</u>
cant<u>a</u>	
mand<u>a</u>	
fum<u>a</u>	
sal<u>a</u>	bonit<u>a</u>
sôp<u>a</u>	car<u>a</u>
bôc<u>a</u>	alt<u>a</u>
mis<u>sa</u>	segund<u>a</u>
vist<u>a</u>	passad<u>a</u>
águ<u>a</u>	barat<u>a</u>
esquin<u>a</u>	fin<u>a</u>
gôt<u>a</u>	fri<u>a</u>

81

FROM SPANISH TO PORTUGUESE

2. Portuguese weak-stressed _i_ sound (as underlined). (See Part I, pages 4-7.)

beb_e_	tom_e_
com_e_	pagu_e_
vend_e_	pass_e_
cab_e_	mud_e_
respond_e_	compr_e_
val_e_	mand_e_
ba_se_	fa_se_
bilhet_e_	qu_e_
tard_e_	es_se_
part_e_	êst_e_
ment_e_	grav_e_
tanqu_e_	verd_e_

FROM SPANISH TO PORTUGUESE

3. Portuguese weak stressed u sound (as underlined). (See Part I, pages 4-7.)

beb<u>o</u>	bonit<u>o</u>
tom<u>o</u>	lind<u>o</u>
com<u>o</u>	car<u>o</u>
ab<u>ro</u>	barat<u>o</u>
pas<u>so</u>	alt<u>o</u>
pa<u>go</u>	segund<u>o</u>
comp<u>ro</u>	quint<u>o</u>
di<u>go</u>	fin<u>o</u>
si<u>go</u>	out<u>ro</u>
vend<u>o</u>	cin<u>co</u>
permit<u>o</u>	quat<u>ro</u>
vam<u>os</u>	fri<u>o</u>
tomam<u>os</u>	sapat<u>o</u>
passam<u>os</u>	minut<u>o</u>
pagam<u>os</u>	ban<u>co</u>
bebem<u>os</u>	mecâni<u>co</u>
comem<u>os</u>	númer<u>o</u>
abrim<u>os</u>	liv<u>ro</u>

The nasal diphthong ãu (as underlined). (See Part I, page 18.)

a. **Unstressed**

(Present)	(Imperfect)
pass**am**	passav**am**
tom**am**	tomav**am**
pag**am**	pagav**am**
compr**am**	compravam
mud**am**	mudav**am**
mand**am**	mandav**am**
visit**am**	visitav**am**
fum**am**	fumav**am**

(Preterite)	(Conditional)
passar**am**	passari**am**
tomar**am**	tomari**am**
pagar**am**	pagari**am**
comprar**am**	comprari**am**
abrir**am**	abriri**am**
seguir**am**	seguiri**am**
perder**am**	perderi**am**
beber**am**	beberi**am**

b. **Stressed**

(Future)

passar**ão**	seguir**ão**
tomar**ão**	abrir**ão**
pagar**ão**	perder**ão**
comprar**ão**	beber**ão**

FROM SPANISH TO PORTUGUESE

5. The unstressed nasal diphthong **ãu** contrasted with the unstressed diphthong **ẽi**. (See Part I, pages 18, 19; also refer to future subjunctive and personal infinitive, Part II.)

(Present)   (Present Subjunctive)

passam   passem
tomam   tomem
pagam   paguem
compram   comprem
visitam   visitem
mandam   mandem

abrem   abram
vendem   vendam
vivem   vivam
bebem   bebam

(Preterite)   (Future Subjunctive and Personal Infinitive)

passaram   passarem
tomaram   tomarem
pagaram   pagarem
compraram   comprarem
mandaram   mandarem
visitaram   visitarem
abriram   abrirem
seguiram   seguirem
perderam   perderem
beberam   beberem

85

FROM SPANISH TO PORTUGUESE

6. The stressed nasal diphthongs **ão** and **õi**. (See Part I, pages 1ʰ, 19.)

lim**ão**	lim**õe**s
mel**ão**	mel**õe**s
mont**ão**	mont**õe**s
sal**ão**	sal**õe**s
cora**ção**	cora**çõe**s
condi**ção**	condi**çõe**s
destina**ção**	destina**çõe**s
se**ção**	se**çõe**s
li**ção**	li**çõe**s
raz**ão**	raz**õe**s
a**ção**	a**çõe**s
invas**ão**	invas**õe**s
miss**ão**	miss**õe**s
ladr**ão**	ladr**õe**s
dire**ção**	dire**çõe**s

7. The diphthongs **ei** and **ou** in preterite verb forms. (See Part I, page 17.)

pass**ei**	pass**ou**
tom**ei**	tom**ou**
pagu**ei**	pag**ou**
mand**ei**	mand**ou**
mud**ei**	mud**ou**
compr**ei**	compr**ou**
fum**ei**	fum**ou**
cant**ei**	cant**ou**
visit**ei**	visit**ou**
fal**ei**	fal**ou**

FROM SPANISH TO PORTUGUESE

8. The diphthongs **eu** and **iu** in preterite verb forms, 3rd person singular. (See Part I, page 17)

parec**eu**	abr**iu**
val**eu**	ped**iu**
com**eu**	segu**iu**
beb**eu**	durm**iu**
vend**eu**	vest**iu**
escrev**eu**	ment**iu**
viv**eu**	v**iu**
d**eu**	prefer**iu**
dev**eu**	resist**iu**

9. Portuguese **b** and **v** sounds. The **b** and **v** are to be pronounced as they are in English. (See Part I, pages 21, 22; also page 26.)

beba	ver	civil
cuba	vaca	palavra
bôba	voz	revista
tubo	valor	passava
subo	valer	pagava
subir	vender	tomava
caber	vários	mandava
receber	ave	estava
roubar	uva	colaborava
cobrar	nôvo	vai, vou, vamos
pobre	dever	vela, bela
obra	viver	
cabeça	escrever	

10. Portuguese d. The d is to be pronounced as it is in English. (See Part I, pages 21, 22).

nada	adulto
cada	idéia
ida	válido
vida	sólida
dedo	resfriado
lado	modêlo
modo	pedido
todo	parado
dado	vestido
pedir	estado
poder	tomado
mudar	entrada
candidato	saída
universidade	unida

FROM SPANISH TO PORTUGUESE

11. Portuguese z sound between vowels. The underlined consonants should all be pronounced with a z sound. The Spanish cognates have an s sound. (See Part I, page ..7.)

a. Within words.

ca<u>s</u>a	a<u>z</u>ul
coi<u>s</u>a	fa<u>z</u>er
me<u>s</u>a	ro<u>z</u>ar
blu<u>s</u>a	<u>z</u>ona
cami<u>s</u>a	va<u>z</u>io
fra<u>s</u>e	<u>z</u>ero
espô<u>s</u>o	ra<u>z</u>ão
espô<u>s</u>a	on<u>z</u>e
u<u>s</u>ar	do<u>z</u>e
acu<u>s</u>ar	tre<u>z</u>e
abu<u>s</u>ar	cator<u>z</u>e
pe<u>s</u>ar	quin<u>z</u>e
ca<u>s</u>ar	pobre<u>z</u>a
pi<u>s</u>ar	triste<u>z</u>a
Bra<u>s</u>il	fortale<u>z</u>a
atra<u>s</u>ado	firme<u>z</u>a
amoro<u>s</u>o	rique<u>z</u>a
fabulo<u>s</u>o	
famo<u>s</u>o	
maravilho<u>s</u>o	
portugue<u>s</u>a	
france<u>s</u>a	
inglê<u>s</u>a	

paí<u>s</u>es	vê<u>z</u>es
me<u>s</u>es	lu<u>z</u>es
inglê<u>s</u>es	feli<u>z</u>es
francê<u>s</u>es	cru<u>z</u>es

FROM SPANISH TO PORTUGUESE

b. Across word boundaries

estamos aqui
comemos aqui
visitamos aqui

vamos entrar
vamos esperar
vamos estar

mais ou menos
mais interessante
menos interessante

vamos a Lima
vamos outra vez
vamos agora

podemos ir
podemos andar
podemos estar

visitamos o país
tomamos outro
nos encontramos aqui

os americanos
os amigos
os espôsos

as americanas
as amigas
as espôsas

os Estados Unidos

12. The Portuguese L sound in close cognates. (See Part I, Pages 24-25.)

sel
sal
tal
mal
qual
mil
papel
hotel
Brasil
abril
civil

falso
falta
alta
alma
solteiro
último
alguma
delgado
Olga
bôlsa
Silva

FROM SPANISH TO PORTUGUESE

nacional   vulgar
espanhol   belga

fácil
difícil
útil
ágil

13. The Portuguese R sound in close cognates. (See Part I, pages 23, 24).

rio   dar
rico   ir
repita   ser
revista   estar
rádio   ver
rápido   tomar
roupa   passar
rei   pagar
remeter   comer
reclamar   beber

barba   guerra
largo   corrida
carne   corra
carta   carro
tarde   tôrre
quarto   arroz
Carlos   cigarro
gordo   barro
verde   fôrro
terceiro   barril
firme   burro

91

www.ingramcontent.com/pod-product-compliance
Lightning Source LLC
Chambersburg PA
CBHW032303150426
43195CB00008BA/558